ATTITUDE · RESOURCE · THEOLOGY

THE A.R.T.
OF SURVIVAL
IN AN AGE OF CHAOS

CHIPINGRAM

ISBN: 978-1-60593-402-0

CONTENTS

INTRODUCTION

We live in an unsettled world. That's nothing new, of course. It's always been so. But certain periods seem more chaotic than others, and recent national and global events have shaken people deeply.

We get unsettled for personal reasons too. We each face crises in certain seasons of life, and some of them can be very traumatic. We have relational struggles, financial problems, health issues, and many other challenges that shake our faith and often seem impossible to overcome. Life can be really difficult sometimes.

As Christians, we know we are called to be overcomers— that the gospel promises victory, not victimhood. But sometimes our biggest question isn't how we can thrive; it's how we can even survive. If we don't have food, money, health, relational connections, and the encouragement and affirmation we need, we start to ask, "Why, Lord?" We wonder why we're going through such a hard time.

There's an art to survival, and the Bible trains us in it. The Church was birthed in desperate times, and one of the earliest letters of the New Testament addresses the difficulties its members were experiencing. The letter was written by James, the half brother of Jesus, to believers who had been scattered by persecution. They needed to know how to survive.

James gives them—and us—answers. I call his teaching at the beginning of his letter the A.R.T. of Survival because it shows us an **A**ttitude to embrace, a **R**esource to ask for, and a **T**heology to believe. When we choose that attitude, receive that resource, and learn to see from the right perspective, we can face any difficult situation with confidence.

Before we dig into James's remarkable passage, let's review some background about the world we live in. The Bible tells us that it's fallen, and even though we've all experienced the resulting frustrations, we're still sometimes surprised by the challenges we face. But Peter told his readers not to be surprised at their painful trials as if they were something strange (1 Peter 4:12). Jesus told His followers that they would have tribulation in the world but not to fear: He had overcome the world (John 16:33). And Paul gave Timothy a promise virtually no one longs to claim: "Everyone who wants to live a godly life in Christ Jesus will be persecuted" (2 Timothy 3:12). Desperate times are not unusual in a fallen world.

So that's the context for our trials, and because of the kind of world we live in, we need to keep three observations in mind as we explore James's teaching:

1. Trials are inevitable. Difficulty in a fallen world is a certainty. In fact, God has subjected us to futility and frustration specifically so we would not get comfortable with sin but seek Him instead (Romans 8:20-21). Our need is a necessary step in His redemption plan.

2. Trials either make us or break us. In Chinese Mandarin, the word for crisis is a combination of the words for tragedy and opportunity. We can look at any crisis as either an insurmountable problem or a great opportunity. Suffering has an uncanny way of driving people away from God *or* driving them toward Him. It sets up critical moments in our lives. We see this throughout the Bible in the stories of characters who chose faith and trust in their most difficult situations as well as in stories of those who compromised or gave up. The fires of our trials can either burn up our faith or purify it into something imperishable.

3. Victims fail to move beyond asking why and remain stuck in their pain. The opposite of a survivor is a victim, and even though our "why" questions are normal and natural, victims get stuck in them. They never get past "Why me, Lord?" and "Why now?" I know how hard it is to put those questions aside— I've asked them when I've been broke, when I've had challenges with my children, when I've been betrayed by people I trusted, when my wife had cancer, or when I've had health issues of my own—but survivors can't stay focused on their pain.

Survivors have other options. The Holy Spirit inspired James to reveal them to us. God's solutions are practical, powerful, and life-changing, and they give us everything we need to remain anchored in eternity in an unsettled world. Let's look at the A.R.T. of Survival!

AN ATTITUDE TO EMBRACE

Anti-Christian persecution broke out more than once in Jerusalem in the years after Jesus's crucifixion (Acts 8:1-3; 11:19; 12:1-4), and many Jewish Christians fled the city. Some stayed behind and likely suffered ongoing persecution; others settled in nearby towns or even more distant cities around the Eastern Mediterranean. Vulnerable to unethical treatment and abuses in their new homes—cut off from family, disinherited, suffering economic hardship—they lived under constant pressure. They were in a desperate situation.

These Christians knew they had eternal life, of course. They had believed in Jesus and experienced His love, grace, and power. Still, they were faced with the here and now of their daily lives. They had to have wondered,

How will we survive these difficulties? How will we handle the pressure? What are we going to do?

You've probably had many of those questions in difficult times too. Looking forward to a glorious eternity with Jesus is wonderfully encouraging, but it doesn't eliminate your hardships today. It doesn't make you immune to all diseases, smooth out your relationships, and pay the bills this month. As much as we rejoice in the big picture, we still can get really stressed out as we go through challenging, exhausting and confusing seasons of life.

The epistle of James was written specifically for those seasons. Imagine Jesus walking into the room in the midst of your desperate situation and you being able to look Him in the eye and ask Him your most pressing questions: *Jesus, what do I do? How do I handle this situation with my family? What do You have to say about my health issue? What if I lose my business? What does the future hold? Where do I go from here?*

James, who pastored the Jerusalem church and was inspired by the Holy Spirit to write this letter to hurting believers, provides Christlike responses to these questions. He gives a brief greeting and launches immediately into some vital instructions:

Consider it pure joy, my brothers and sisters, whenever you face trials of many kinds, because you know that the testing of your faith produces perseverance. Let perseverance finish its work so that you may be mature and complete, not lacking anything. (James 1:2-4)

Many scholars believe this is one of the earliest books of the New Testament. James is writing to a primarily Jewish audience—Jews who have believed in Jesus as the Messiah and now feel as if their world is falling apart. And the first instruction he gives them is not about the right thing to do or the right words to say. It's about an attitude to have: "Consider it pure joy."

Don't mistake this directive for an encouraging pat on the back. It is given as a command, not a recommendation, and it's followed by a reminder of how God works in our lives. The testing of faith produces perseverance, which leads to maturity and completeness. We get to learn by experience that trials lead to really good outcomes.

That amazing principle leads to a second command: "Let perseverance finish its work." In other words, don't give up. Don't become a victim. God promises that in Christ, we are more than conquerors (Romans 8:37).

But we don't get to experience the joy of that victory if we don't begin with the right attitude.

Victims ask why, and survivors ask what.

Victims and survivors have different attitudes. The cry of a victim is, "Why?" It's a legitimate question, but it rarely leads to answers. God doesn't give us the why behind everything that happens in our lives, but He does give us the answer to another question: "What?" Regardless of the issue—a cancer diagnosis, a crippling economic burden, a fearsome pandemic, a relational crisis—victims approach it with one kind of attitude, while survivors and overcomers approach it with another. Victims ask why, and survivors ask what. If we want to survive our challenges and even thrive during them, we will need to learn the right questions to ask.

Three Important "What" Questions

Those who survive and thrive in crises learn to ask three very important "what" questions, and each of them is answered in James 1:2-4. God will empower you, by His Spirit, to be a survivor, overcomer, and conqueror of whatever you're facing as you follow the instructions in this passage in the context of fellowship with other believers.

Question 1: What can I control when my world falls apart?

You probably can't control your circumstances. You also probably can't control the reactions and behavior of people around you. And you certainly can't control national or global events or the leaders who make decisions about them. But you do have complete control over at least one thing: your attitude. You can choose how to respond internally before you ever do anything externally.

In case you're wondering, James is not talking just about inconveniences here; he's talking about painful, overwhelming trials. How in the world are we supposed to consider it pure joy when we are, as James's words say, surrounded by these trials? Yet because the Spirit of the all-powerful, all-knowing God—the One who lives above all circumstances and is never defeated by anything—is inside us, we can live above circumstances too. We can trust that even when we can't get past our immediate problems, God is going to work everything out for our good. The testing of our faith is going to produce something valuable and everlasting. We can go ahead and rejoice in that promise even before we see it fulfilled.

So the answer to this first "what" question is your *attitude*. That's the focus. Don't confuse attitude with feelings. You may not feel joyful in the thick of life's painful challenges, but you can still choose joy. You can choose to approach your challenges with the attitude that whatever is happening today, God will turn it into good at some point in the future. Your faith will be tested and come out stronger. And that is worth rejoicing over.

You may have to fight for that joy. You've probably discovered that pity parties don't accomplish very much. They don't even help you feel better. But putting on the full armor of God (Ephesians 6:10-20), recognizing that the One who is in you is greater than anything in the world (1 John 4:4), and insisting that God has not given you a spirit of fear (2 Timothy 1:7) can empower you. You grab hold of the anchor of hope and refuse to give up. Moment by moment, you choose your attitude.

Question 2: What must I do to make it through today?

Much of our distress in a crisis comes from looking at tomorrow and wondering how it could possibly work out well. *What will happen next month? What will happen in my business? My church? Our country? I can't see any way out.*

Very quickly, our minds can play out all sorts of implications and possibilities for the future, and those possibilities easily turn into likelihoods. But God hasn't told us to figure out tomorrow. He hasn't given us grace for the future yet. He has given us grace for today. Our job is to depend on that grace to make it through this day alone, each and every day.

The answer to this second "what" question is simple: *endure.* Just as we make a choice to consider it all joy, we choose to persevere. We say, "I won't give in. I won't give up. I won't become a victim. I'm in it for as long as it takes."

I have read about James Stockdale, a Navy officer and aviator who spent nearly eight years as a prisoner of war during Vietnam in the brutal war camp known as the Hanoi Hilton. Stockdale, who was given the Medal of Honor when he came home, was asked how he survived and why some POWs made it and some didn't. He had a ready answer. The optimists died, he said. Optimism itself wasn't the problem—generally it's a good attitude to have—but in this situation, it set up false expectations. The prisoners who counted on quickly being freed sunk into despair. They lost their focus on endurance and gave up.

James says that the testing of faith does the opposite for those who believe. It sharpens your focus. It produces perseverance. It won't necessarily lighten the load of your difficulties. In fact, you can be under enormous emotional, relational, financial, or circumstantial stress, looking at the situation around you without any idea of how it's going to work out, fully aware of your desperation, yet still cling tenaciously to the goodness of God. Even in the midst of your most intense crisis, His grace is sufficient for each and every moment.

Like being joyful, enduring is a choice. The more we do it, the stronger we get. Just as the fibers of weightlifters' muscles get torn apart in a workout only to grow back stronger and bigger before the next one, our faith is pulled, stretched, and shredded every time we have to endure something. That builds strength for the next time. God very often takes our faith beyond its normal capacity, knowing that it will heal, expand, and be fortified in the process.

You don't have to know how you'll handle tomorrow's problems; you just need to realize that God's power is perfected in your weakness and that regardless of what you'll face in the future, you'll have the grace to deal with it. God will show up. And because having faith counts on that fact, you can persevere today and even let your heart be at rest in Him.

You'll find that whenever you start thinking about tomorrow's problems, the grace to endure seems to vanish. But when you choose not to give up today— and make that choice one day at a time, or even one moment at a time, if necessary—grace holds you up.

When the dot-com bubble burst in the late 1990s, the market crashed and took a painfully long time to recover. At the time, I was leading a global ministry that funded work all over the world. Our budget was millions of dollars, and suddenly the supply shut down. Leaders in various countries were depending on our support, and we had no resources to send them. I didn't know what to do. It was a devastating and seemingly hopeless situation.

But those leaders all over the world found innovative ways to continue their ministries on a fraction of the budget. Our work actually expanded into more countries. I learned that a crisis can be God's way of changing things for long-term growth and effectiveness. Endurance is a heavy price to pay in situations like that, but, as in everything with God, the benefits at the end far outweigh the cost of the process. Those who endure are rewarded by God with great works *for* them, *in* them, and *through* them.

Throughout Scripture, great men and women of faith learned from overwhelming difficulties, pain, and injustices to cling to God's promises. When you grab His invisible promises and hold them dear, choosing to obey and trust when you have no idea how things will work out, God shows up. That's His promise for those who endure.

Question 3: What hope do I have for tomorrow?

Hope is said to be the oxygen of the soul. If we don't have it, we won't choose joy in our trials and won't be able to persevere through them. Hope lifts us out from under our circumstances and gives us the view above and beyond them. We need it in every situation in life.

So what's the answer to this "what" question? Where do we get hope? We accept the fact—the promise of God—that He will take the worst we experience today and use it for good. He always has our best in mind. He can take the most difficult, desperate, painful situations in our lives, work them into His purposes, and turn them to our advantage.

That doesn't mean God will immediately change our circumstances. Hope isn't based on avoiding the processes we're going through. Some misguided theologies teach that if we are obedient to God and pray and believe all the right things, everything will go our way. That leads to disillusionment.

It's true that everything will work out for our good— that's the promise of Romans 8:28—but not everything will be problem-free. Our "why" questions about the things that are happening to us aren't answered that easily. This is what James means when he says to let perseverance finish its work so we may be mature and complete, "not lacking anything" (James 1:4). Embracing joy, enduring, and choosing hope is how we cooperate with God in His process of bringing us to perfection.

That's essentially what James's words mean. *Teleios*, often translated as "perfect" or "mature" in verse 4, refers not to sinless perfection but to the "perfecting," or fulfillment, of our design. God's purpose for you is to make you like Jesus. Romans 8:28, the verse we so often quote about God working everything together for our good, leads to the same conclusion. The very next verse says, "Those God foreknew he also predestined to be conformed to the image of his Son." When we place our hope in God's purposes for our lives, we give Him room to fulfill our design and mature us.

The result is that we are "not lacking anything." I vividly remember crying out to God in my most desperate situations and thinking about how much I was lacking: *Lord, I've taken huge steps of faith and followed You with all my heart, and this is what I get?* He has gently reminded me that my responsibility to Him is not to make my world work out the way I think it should but rather to trust and obey Him—to rest in His plans, even when I don't understand them.

If I ever need a sobering example, I can simply look at the apostles. They served God well. They loved Him with all their hearts. They accomplished great things in the power of His Spirit. And as far as scholars know, every apostle was martyred except John, who was exiled. The book of Hebrews tells us about many heroes of faith who never saw the fulfillment of God's big-picture promises. They simply had to trust. And because they did—because they looked in hope beyond their immediate circumstances—"the world was not worthy of them" (Hebrews 11:38).

Our anchor is not in this temporal world; it's in heaven. The early Church seemed to know this well. Its members were persecuted for not worshipping the emperor, and they often willingly sacrificed their lives to serve others.

When most people fled cities to escape the plagues of the second and third centuries, many believers stayed behind to minister to those who were sick, knowing they might lose their own lives in the process. That's the love of Christ and the hope of eternity at work, and it made a dramatic impression on nonbelievers. By around the middle of the fourth century, nearly half of the sixty million people in the Roman Empire had become followers of Jesus.[1]

God wants you to know that in any crisis, you can control your attitude and choose joy. You can make it through your difficulties by persevering. And you can have hope by knowing that an all-wise, all-powerful, all-loving God is working to bring about the best possible ends, by the best possible means, for the most possible people, for the longest possible time. The threefold approach of joy, endurance, and hope may not change anything about your situation right now, but it changes everything about your view of it. It brings you peace.

The promise later in the first chapter of James puts it all in perspective: "Blessed is the one who perseveres under trial because, having stood the test, that person will receive the crown of life that the Lord has promised to those who love him" (verse 12). God gives strength and grace in the moment and an extravagant reward in the end. Fixing our eyes on that prize and on the Savior who promises it, we find mercy in our time of need.

A Perspective on Pain

If you are going through adversity, difficulty, pain, or other challenges, I would encourage you to look at your trials through a biblical lens. We usually see trials with distorted vision when we're going through them, but God's view is different from ours, and embracing His truth helps us see clearly from an eternal perspective. The following five biblical observations will help you see your challenges from that vantage point.

1. God uses adversity to make us mature because we are forced to <u>depend</u> on Him at a new level.
I'm not saying that God is the author of our adversity, but He does use the misfortune we face for specific purposes. Left to ourselves, we tend toward self-sufficiency and pride and become insensitive to Him. Trials remind us of how completely dependent we are on Him.

2. We are <u>weaned</u> from the temporal and urgent affairs of life and forced to reexamine our values, priorities, commitments, and future.

When we go through trying times, we have to deal with difficult questions: *What am I living for? What really matters? What am I giving my life to?* God speaks to us in those questions, and we become especially sensitive to His voice when we are desperate to hear Him. Trials put us in that position.

3. Trials allow us to <u>witness</u> firsthand the reality and power of God.

Our need becomes the vehicle of God's grace, and our problems become the object of His power. When we are put in a position of having to trust God, we see His supernatural power like never before. When we need provision, we see Him as our Provider. When we are in danger, we see Him as our Protector. When we are sick, we see Him as our Healer. We lean into the specific aspect of His nature that we most need. Our self-pity does not reveal His nature to us, but our trust in His presence and power does. The Spirit of God that raised

> Our need becomes the vehicle of God's grace, and our problems become the object of His power.

Christ from the dead is at work in us, and we get to see that in times of need. He alone is our hope.

4. Trials serve as an awesome <u>testimony</u> to an unbelieving world.

The way we endure hardship makes a statement. It shows the world how real God is. I recently spent an afternoon with a man whose wife had undergone numerous treatments for cancer. He had been steadfast in prayer and faith throughout the ordeal but was concerned about what kind of testimony he would have if his wife died. Would his trust in God prove to be unfounded?

I assured him that his testimony was based not on whether his wife lived or died but rather on the power and presence of God in their lives as they went through this hardship. Their attitude was a testimony in itself. His love reflected God's love. Her faith and endurance were powerful evidence of God's work in her.

Like Paul and Silas singing hymns while they were in prison (Acts 16:25), not yet knowing the outcome, this couple pointed to God's goodness regardless of their circumstances. That kind of response in trials is unexplainable in the world's eyes. It's a wonderful testimony that one way or another makes God's power visible.

5. We <u>become</u> sensitive, caring, compassionate, Christlike people.

People who have been hurt deeply usually know how to love deeply. Our trials don't last forever, but the kindness, tenderness, and compassion they produce do. As long as we don't allow ourselves to become bitter, we come out equipped and empowered to love other people at their point of need—just like Jesus does.

A lot of lasting fruit comes from learning how to ask "what" rather than "why" in the midst of a trial. We become trained in the art of perspective—able to experience joy, endure, and be filled with hope. We become mature and complete, lacking in nothing. We receive all that God promises to give us each moment of every day. And we become living, lasting testimonies of His presence and power.

[1] Rodney Stark, *The Rise of Christianity: How the Obscure, Marginal Jesus Movement Became the Dominant Religious Force in the Western World in a Few Centuries* (San Francisco: Harper San Francisco, 1997), 5-7, 73-94.

A RESOURCE TO ASK FOR

Jerry was an amazing athlete. By all accounts, he had a wonderful (and lucrative) football career ahead of him. But walking downtown with his girlfriend one night, he saw two guys who had just come out of a bar fighting with each other, and when one of them pulled out a knife, Jerry instinctively stepped between them.

Jerry managed to separate the two men, but one had a gun, and Jerry ended up with two bullets in his back. He was paralyzed. His career, along with all the potential fame and millions of dollars that came with it, was over before it started.

Jerry believed in God, but he didn't claim to have a close relationship with Him at the time. Over and over again, he asked, "Why me, God? I don't understand." If anyone had a right to ask why—to wonder why God would allow that when he was doing the right thing by trying to save a life—Jerry did.

Jerry noticed two kinds of people in rehab. "I watched people who kept asking why. They focused inward and wallowed in self-pity. They made little progress, and their lives crumbled. But a few people—very few—simply focused on what they needed to do to get better. They felt devastated too, but they looked for hope and tried to make it through each day. Those are the ones who succeeded."

I learned later that Jerry had become a Paralympics gold-medalist basketball player and marathoner. Even after his tragedy, he was a fabulous athlete, but only because he learned how to hang in there even when he didn't feel any hope. He learned the A.R.T. of Survival.

We've seen that survivors make it through the most devastating crises by asking three "what" questions. *What can I control?* **My attitude.** *What must I do to make it through today?* **Endure.** *What hope do I have for tomorrow?* ***An all-powerful, all-knowing God promises to take the worst I experience in this life and turn it around for my good, either in this life or in heaven.***

Jerry learned to stop asking the "why" questions, began asking the "what" questions, and focused on the opportunity in front of him. If God allowed Jerry's crisis to happen, He had a plan for it, so Jerry went into training and became a world-class athlete again. He also ended up with an amazing testimony that he shared across America and around the world, of how the supernatural power of God at work within him changed his life. In addition, Jerry partnered with ministries that delivered wheelchairs to the poorest of the poor.

Jerry once confided in me that if he could go back and live that part of his life over again, he wouldn't change a thing. He said,

> Do I like sitting in this chair? No. I thought money and fame were my ticket to the good life, but intimacy with Christ is life. I have His peace, joy, and power, and God has used me to change other people's lives all over the world. I became a survivor instead of a victim because He gave me hope. And instead of kind of believing in God, I became a genuine follower of Jesus. I wouldn't trade that for anything.

Of course, the long version of Jerry's story has many setbacks and times of being stuck in depression. But the point is, what matters is not the ups and downs we experience—everybody has those—but rather the direction we choose.

When you're discouraged about serious challenges with work, health, finances, depression, relationships, kids, or any other crisis life throws at you, you can still choose joy, you can still endure, and you can still recognize God's intention to work everything out for your good.

But that doesn't mean you have to fake it. There will be times when you don't feel joyful, you want to give up, and you aren't sure God even has a plan. That's probably why James makes a significant shift in verse 5. Having told us to choose our attitude, persevere, and trust God's process, he points us toward a valuable resource. Whenever we get stuck and don't know what to do, God wants to give us a priceless gift. He wants to show us exactly what to do 100 percent of the time.

What to Do When You're Stuck

James continues with a sweeping promise:

> If any of you lacks wisdom, you should ask God, who gives generously to all without finding fault, and it will be given to you. But when you ask, you must believe and not doubt, because the one who doubts is like a wave of the sea, blown and tossed by the wind. That person should not expect to receive anything from the Lord. Such a person is double-minded and unstable in all they do. (James 1:5-8)

What do you do when you're stuck in your pain? How do you keep going in the middle of a crisis when you feel like giving up? What do you do when emotional, financial, relational, or health issues are swirling around and no matter how eager you are to follow God, you don't know how? Those are the questions James is addressing here.

God understands when we get stuck. He knows how much we need His direction when we don't know what to do. So, through James, He gives us a wonderful offer that comes with one condition to follow in order to receive it. But first, let's discuss the offer.

God's Offer: Supernatural Wisdom

The wisdom God promises us isn't intellectual; it's the ability to know what to do, when to do it, and how to do it in the midst of any situation. This is the Hebrew concept of wisdom—remember that James is writing to Jewish believers—which refers to God's design for life. There's a way to think, decide, carry out our responsibilities, live out our relationships, and follow God that fits His design, and He wants to give us everything we need to develop that skill.

Our Responsibility: We Have to Ask

The Jewish Christians reading James's letter had believed in the Messiah, seen miracles, and experienced transformed lives. Now their lives seemed to be falling apart. So James tells them to ask for God's wisdom and believe they will receive it. He doesn't tell them to try harder or figure it out; he directs them to the source of wisdom and urges them to ask for it.

In this early stage of the church, well-worn Christian platitudes didn't exist yet. James is not just saying, "Pray about it." He instructs his readers to come to God and request a gift in prayer—to say, "Lord, I don't know what to do in this situation, but my eyes are on You. I need You to point me in the right direction. I need the gift of divine wisdom."

God's Attitude When We Come: Open and Generous

The promise that follows the offer and the response is clear: God will give His wisdom generously.

I've been a pastor for more than three decades, and I've seen people stuck in all kinds of issues—with seemingly impossible relational, financial, legal, and health problems. I've been amazed at how many Christians will do almost anything in those crises to figure out what they ought to do except ask God in genuine humility for His wisdom.

That used to puzzle me, but I think I understand now. Many people have a warped view of God and assume that when they need His help the most, He'll probably stand there with His arms crossed and point out where they messed up. Most people have a nagging conscience about their own sins—those indiscretions, those rationalizations, those times of willful disobedience—and many think their sins will interfere with their prayers and their ability to receive direction from God.

Notice what James writes: God "gives generously to all without finding fault." His words literally mean, "Come to the gift-giving God." God is a Father who understands when His children make mistakes or even go through times of keeping their distance from Him. He never says, "Clean yourself up before you come to Me"; He simply wants us to come, just as we are. When we recognize that we can't make it without Him and go to Him for help, He's there. He gives generously. That's who He is.

I love the phrase "without finding fault." Some translations say "without reproach." There's no rebuke waiting for us when we go to Him for wisdom. His arms aren't crossed, He isn't pointing His finger at us, and He isn't holding out on us. He eagerly invites us because He is kind, good, understanding, and extremely loving.

That's why Jesus encourages those who are weary and burdened to go to Him. It's why He taught His disciples to pray using a very familiar term for father: *abba*, meaning papa or daddy. He makes it clear that the Father's arms are open.

When people go through difficult times, they often blame their circumstances, the people who haven't treated them right, the government, the culture, or anything other than themselves. But deep down, they are carrying guilt. They are turning their inward blame outward. God wants us to know that there's no need to pull away from Him. He wants us to go and ask for the guidance we need.

The One Condition

There's one very important condition that comes with God's offer, and it breaks down into two parts: "You must believe and not doubt" (verse 6). First, we have to ask in faith, and, second, our faith can't be mixed with doubt.

How is that possible? Let's start by looking at what it means to ask in faith. This does not mean a tentative request, hoping God might possibly answer and, if He does, that we might think about following His advice. It means trusting Him, having confidence in His character and His Word, and committing to doing what He shows us. It also means recognizing that He's the sovereign God of the universe and has every right to lead us as He desires and expect us to follow.

Then we ask without doubting. Some people get tripped up on this condition and think it means that even a moment of questioning disqualifies us from an answer. The doubt James refers to here is not the concern we have sometimes about whether God is really going to take care of us, or that subtle feeling that even though He *can* come through, He might have other purposes. God knows we're human, and He understands the struggles we have. Intellectual doubts are common, and they don't disqualify us from answers. That's not the kind of doubt James is talking about.

The doubt in this passage is about disloyalty. James describes what this doubt looks like: someone who "is like a wave of the sea, blown and tossed by the wind" (verse 6). That kind of doubt makes a person "double-minded" (verse 8), or two-souled. It's the same word we get *schizophrenia* from. The picture is of someone who prays to know God's will as a matter of information, something to consider, without any commitment to following it. It's a "we'll see" kind of prayer. Once God gives His wisdom, this person then evaluates it and decides whether or not to follow it.

That kind of prayer gets a predictable response: "That person should not expect to receive anything from the Lord" (verse 7).

Perhaps that warning seems harsh, especially for people going through a really difficult time. But God always wants to work *in* us before He works *through* us.

When we need His wisdom, He works in us when we go to Him with a request, but it needs to be

> God always wants to work *in* us before He works *through* us.

a particular kind of request: we ask with a heartfelt commitment to our relationship with Him and a conviction that His wisdom is best for us.

Look at it as a blank check from God. He promises to give it to you, but you have to sign the contract first. You ask Him for wisdom about where to live, how to handle your debt, how to survive a job loss, how to manage your health crisis, what to do when all doors are closed, how to make it through today, or whatever your conundrum is. When you commit up front, by faith, to do whatever He says, He promises to show up 100 percent of the time with His wisdom and direction.

Not long after Theresa and I got married, we moved away to prepare for ministry. Both of our fathers were alcoholics, we came from dysfunctional families, and we still thought everything would work out just fine because we loved Jesus. But six months after our wedding, while I was in seminary, our marriage wasn't working. We didn't know how to resolve conflict, we made each other crazy, and sometimes we wouldn't talk to each other for a couple of days.

I felt really guilty that I was preparing for ministry and couldn't even manage my marriage. No matter how hard I tried to do it right, nothing worked. I came to chapter 1 of James and said, "Lord, I can't fix this. Will You show me what to do? Whatever it is, I'll do it." And while my head was bowed and my hands were lifted up, I heard the Holy Spirit say, "Go to a good Christian counselor."

That was not at all what I wanted to hear. Counseling was for people with *real* needs, and I'd be very embarrassed for anyone to know we had a problem. But when the Spirit whispered, "Is your pride getting in the way?" I had to admit that it was.

I think many of us ask God for wisdom while assuming that it will fit within a certain box of acceptability. Very often, it doesn't. If we're serious about seeking His wisdom, we have to be ready to follow wherever He leads.

When we approach God with that commitment, He gives His wisdom generously. I could tell story after story of how He came through when I most needed to hear from Him.

He once led me to relocate to the other side of the country, even when I had all kinds of reasons it wouldn't be a good idea. Early in our ministry, my wife and I sat in the middle of the living room after a week of eating just vegetables and prayed for food, asking God for His wisdom on how to get by with the ten dollars we had left. One day, Theresa came home after dropping the kids off at school and found five bags of groceries on our front porch. They were filled with meat, cheese, and the exact same kind of flour she used to make bread. We had gone at least a couple of weeks without some of these things, and we had not told a single person that we had any needs. But God knew, and He came through. (I believe in angels.)

Another time, we were completely out of money and couldn't pay our rent, so I asked God for wisdom and provision. I went to the mailbox the next day and found a check from a man I hadn't heard from or even thought about for years. He had attended just one hour of a Bible study I'd taught when he was in high school. He went on to get drafted by the Green Bay Packers. God woke him up one night and put my name on his mind. I'll never forget opening the envelope with a Packers logo on it, wondering who in the world it could be from, and inside was a check for a thousand dollars.

This kind of supernatural intervention isn't just for a select few who get to experience a rare demonstration of God's goodness. It's for anyone, especially those who are in a desperate situation and go to Him with humility and a commitment to follow Him. In other words, it's for you.

That doesn't mean God's wisdom will be easy to follow. It may not be comfortable or convenient. It may be a minor adjustment. But if He says to relocate, then do that. If He tells you to forgive someone who has deeply offended you, then forgive. If it involves a career change, an embarrassing confession, a humble apology, or anything else that stretches you out of your comfort zone, don't resist.

He gives His wisdom because it's actually wise. Following it is always a good thing to do.

When you ask for God's wisdom, keep your eyes and ears and heart open. He may show you something through His Word, a book, a sermon, a counselor, a friend, a whisper from the Holy Spirit, or a number of other means. He has a way of putting His wisdom in spiritual neon lights, drawing our attention to it, impressing it upon us, and authenticating it as His voice. He won't whisper it and then blame us for not hearing. If we're attentive, He will be persistent in making it plain.

In Your Time of Need

God doesn't leave you in your quandaries. He will help you get unstuck if you

1. admit you're stuck;
2. recognize you can't do anything on your own;
3. ask Him for supernatural wisdom; and
4. become willing to do whatever His wisdom demands of you.

When you take these four steps in response to His offer, you'll see how He comes through.

God always makes His wisdom available to those who seek Him, but He is especially drawn to us when we're at the end of our rope. A frequent theme throughout Scripture is that He "is close to the brokenhearted and saves those who are crushed in spirit" (Psalm 34:18). He invites us to approach His throne with confidence "so that we may receive mercy and find grace to help us in our time of need" (Hebrews 4:16).

When we're at rock bottom, in a desperate situation, with nowhere else to turn, God promises supernatural wisdom. He'll show us exactly what to do, how to do it, when to do it, and who to do it with if our hearts are open to hearing Him and committed to doing what He says. That's His standing invitation to every one of us.

We will each have different crises and challenges in our lives, but God's invitation in all of them is the same. When circumstances remind us of our dependence on Him and drive us into His Word, we have an opportunity to receive His perspective and see life through new eyes. He longs to give it to us. He wants to impart His wisdom. He simply asks that we receive it without double-mindedness or doubting. He fills in the top of the contract and writes out the blank check. We only have to sign our agreement—our commitment to follow. Then His wisdom flows into our hearts and minds.

When Jesus was in the garden the night before His crucifixion, He prayed, "My Father, if it is possible, may this cup be taken from me. Yet not as I will, but as you will" (Matthew 26:39). That's the kind of surrender that will allow you to receive God's wisdom. When you're in a desperate situation and offer yourself to Him as a living sacrifice, surrendering to His will as your act of spiritual service, you have taken an essential step in the A.R.T. of Survival. When you declare that your future is His, your money is His, your family is His, and your entire life is His, you have put yourself in a position to receive His very best for you.

That's how you survive a crisis. God gives you the most valuable resource in the world: His wisdom. He leads you through your circumstances with enough grace to handle each day and a promise to work everything together for your good. No matter how difficult the first steps are, they are worth it. With God's wisdom, you not only survive but also thrive.

A THEOLOGY TO BELIEVE

An old story tells of Satan going to market and selling the tools he used to blind unbelievers and ruin the faith of Christians who were walking closely with God. All the junior demons were invited to buy these tools for their work in deceiving people—faithful Christians, nominal Christians, and the unbelieving world.

One small box in this sale was tagged with an astronomical price. All the demons marveled. What could possibly be worth so much and fit in that tiny box? They could hardly imagine a tool so valuable.

Satan explained, "That box holds *discouragement*. It's more useful to me than every other tool I've used. With that, I can pry open human hearts, get inside them, and render them powerless. I use it almost all the time, but nobody knows it's coming from me. I deceive people with it, make everything look hopeless, and eventually get them to give up."

That's an amusing story, but it makes a powerful point. Discouragement destroys lives—not in any obvious way, and not immediately, but little by little over time. We can feel it at any moment, but it is especially devastating when crises hit, circumstances are challenging, and hope seems unrealistic. Discouragement makes the problems look enormous and God look small, and sooner or later we feel like giving up.

I can think of many times when I've been discouraged. There have been ministry issues, health issues, family issues, financial downturns, and national or global crises that had an unsettling impact on my life and the lives of my family and church members. In some of those times, I've sought God and prayed like never before, and still things seemed to get worse.

I recently came across a journal I'd written in years ago during one of those very dark times. In it, I saw this excerpt:

For twenty months, I have clung to a passage and a promise in Psalm 25. The journey has been characterized by pain, injustice, betrayal, the stripping of the old, new insights into my pride. We're broke, personally and as a ministry. We have no office, no staff to speak of, no clear direction for teaching, and a future that is uncertain and unknown, and we are forced to live simply by faith and the clear conviction and pain that we must move forward to helping Christians live like Christians with what we have, which is little; with where we are, which is difficult; and with God, who brought us here. I have been tempted many times to give up. I have felt deeply, deeply discouraged. And I have battled feelings of hopelessness in the midst of this journey.

I look back now at what God did in the aftermath of that trial, and I realize He had to do a lot of deep work *in* me before He did some significant work *through* me. I had to learn what the first two chapters of this book have been about: considering it all joy when nothing around me looks joyful. I had to come to the point where I said, *Lord, I don't know what to do. I don't have any money. I don't have direction. Difficulty is at every turn. I need Your wisdom.*

In my case it took me twenty months to understand the work that God was doing both *in* and *through* me.

Slaying the Dragon of Discouragement

By definition, discouragement is about losing courage. When courage rises up within us, we can face the circumstances. We know God is bigger than any mountain in our way. We press forward, confident that we can do all things through Christ, who gives us strength (Philippians 4:13).

Discouragement erodes all that confidence and causes us to lose heart. It slowly convinces us that we're powerless, that nothing will ever change, that there's no point in even trying. It's that feeling that makes compromises, shortcuts, and quitting seem like our most realistic options.

You probably have some experience with that feeling. Most people do, at least in certain seasons of life. So as you read the rest of this chapter, I want you to do so with your most discouraging situation in mind. I believe that if you do that prayerfully, God will speak to you through His Word about that situation and any others you may be facing.

Discouragement is the number one destroyer of God's plans for our lives. If we could see from heaven's perspective, we'd realize that we often throw in the towel just before we were set to receive God's highest and best.

I've seen it again and again when counseling people. Right before a couple is about to learn how to forgive, resolve their issues, and experience a breakthrough in their marriage, they give up and get a divorce. Or a ministry team, right before they're about to receive a huge answer to prayer for open doors or financial support, lose heart and walk away. Or an addict, about to reach a major milestone in breaking free, sinks into despair and lapses back into old habits. It's a painfully consistent pattern.

But God gives us a plan for slaying the dragon of discouragement. When we're wondering how to survive when we're tired, when we've tried as long and hard as we can, when we've prayed and still haven't seen an answer, when everything in us feels like quitting because we just can't take the disappointment anymore, He gives us an answer.

As we've seen, God's plan begins with an attitude: **joyful endurance**. That attitude produces a result: that we would become mature, complete, lacking in nothing. God also gives us an invaluable resource: **supernatural wisdom**.

Now, as we continue in James 1, God gives us **a theology**—a divine perspective, a big-picture truth about life, circumstances, and our future. When this perspective really sinks in, discouragement loses its power:

> Believers in humble circumstances ought to take pride in their high position. But the rich should take pride in their humiliation—since they will pass away like a wild flower. For the sun rises with scorching heat and withers the plant; its blossom falls and its beauty is destroyed. In the same way, the rich will fade away even while they go about their business. Blessed is the one who perseveres under trial because, having stood the test, that person will receive the crown of life that the Lord has promised to those who love him. (James 1:9-12)

God's prescription for our discouragement is a divine perspective. He tells us to look at our lives through the lens of His kingdom. From ground level, the naked eye sees the rich and powerful as the people who have it made. They're secure and comfortable. But in God's kingdom, the opposite is true: those in humble circumstances are in the highest position. And James proceeds to tell us why.

> God's prescription for our discouragement is a divine perspective.

"Believers in humble circumstances" is not a statement on character or attitude; it's a socioeconomic position. Those who don't have very much money should rejoice in their high position.

I have to admit, I found these verses to be challenging when I first studied them long ago. But in years of Bible study, I've discovered that confusing passages that don't seem to make much sense on the surface usually have some profound insights hidden in them somewhere. This is one of those passages.

From heaven's perspective, those who find themselves in very challenging situations are naturally more prone to depend on God, and that's the highest position a human being can be in. When we don't have anything, we automatically turn to Him.

I will never forget another time when we were literally broke. We had no money and no food, and we had moved to a new city. We sat in our car after a church service and prayed for something to eat for lunch—not because we were spiritual or being obedient but because we had nothing. And while we were praying, we heard a knock on our window. Someone who had sat behind us during church wanted to get to know our family and was inviting us home for lunch. We had turned to God in desperation, and He drew near.

People facing difficult challenges are in a better position to become rich in faith than those in ease and comfort are. Not every desperate person turns toward faith (discouragement often casts very dark shadows), but turning to God is instinctive in hard times. When we are socially and economically low, we are positioned to seek God and trust Him. And those who are materially rich—who have enough for today and lots of tomorrows—easily default to spiritual cruise control and forget how to depend on God.

Few middle- and upper-class people today consider themselves rich. But by biblical (and global) standards, if we aren't concerned about having a roof over our heads and what we're going to eat tomorrow, we're very well off. We are the ones James is talking to when he says, "The rich should take pride in their humiliation" (verse 10). Money can be a great asset used for kingdom purposes, but it often puts us at a spiritual disadvantage because it provides false security. It cultivates our idols, sometimes even becoming an idol itself. It convinces many people (even Christians) that they can live life their own way, without God.

In any situation, we need to choose to depend on Him. It doesn't matter how much or how little money we have in the bank. If we don't pray and don't live in complete dependence, we are in a very low and dangerous position. That's James's challenge to the rich and poor alike. Why? Because life is transitory. "The sun rises with scorching heat and withers the plant; its blossom falls and its beauty is destroyed" (verse 11). Our lives pass away like vapors.

I've talked to people recently who had spent decades building their businesses, investing their money, and making their retirement secure. And when the COVID-19 pandemic hit, everything was beaten down. We can't trust in wealth, even when we've used it wisely. It can fade away in an instant.

But "blessed is the one who perseveres" (verse 12). Blessedness is an inner quality of happiness independent of circumstances. Those who persevere are happy. And *perseveres* is the same word we saw in verses 3 and 4. The testing of our faith produces endurance, and this endurance leads to blessedness.

Or, to paraphrase James, "Happy is the person who refuses to give up and chooses to trust God even under stress and pressure, even when discouraged, even with vanishing finances or poor health, even under extreme spiritual opposition." Having passed that test, "that person will receive the crown of life" (verse 12).

What does it mean to pass the test? It means being faithful to your calling, not giving up, not giving in to temptation, not compromising, not throwing in the towel on your assignment from God. Whether the difficult situation is with a spouse or child or boss, you hang in there.

That kind of perseverance brings the crown of life—in other words, "the crown, which is life." The crown is life itself. We do get rewards in heaven—Jesus was clear about that—but this promise is bigger and better. It's about abundant life now *and* forever.

When you refuse to let discouragement sabotage you, you get a certain quality of life in return: a closeness with Jesus that brings courage, faith, power, and experiences that other people don't get. You receive life now and future rewards that God has promised to those who love Him and who remain loyal to Him no matter how difficult the circumstances become.

Hanging Tough in Tough Times

I believe this passage in James contains three powerful, practical principles that can help slay the dragon of discouragement.

1. Get God's perspective on your <u>circumstances</u>.

How? By looking at circumstances through the eyes of *faith*. First, recognize what is actually causing your discouragement. What is causing you to think, *I just can't take it anymore*? Through the eyes of faith, seek to see what God is going to do in response to your trust in His character and promises.

How do you do that? You need to understand that God has put you in a position to do a work in you that is more important than the work itself. When I wrote that I'd been clinging to a promise in Psalm 25 for twenty months, I believed He would instruct me in the way I should go (verse 12). Every day God gave me the guidance I needed for only that day. I kept asking Him for the ten-year vision, the five-year vision, even the six-month plan, but He gave me grace for only today.

> When God is going to do something wide through you, He has to do something deep in you.

I didn't realize then that God had bigger and deeper purposes for my marriage, children, grandchildren, and ministry that would expand and increase His influence through us. But when God is going to do something wide through you, He has to do something deep in you. And to do something deep in you, He has to remove your false dependencies: pride, trust in other people, the affirmation of others, or whatever else you count on. He strips us of our false props not because He is down on us but because we are precious to Him. It's a painful process, but it's good.

I would love to be able to tell you that when everything is going well, when your relationships are solid and you have plenty of provision, you will go to deep places with God if you just trust Him. That may be true, but it usually isn't. Even when really godly people seem to have it all together on the outside, they've faced some really challenging circumstances few people know about. Some trial or another caused them enormous suffering. We all have had seasons when God takes the things we trust and sets them aside so we have nothing but Him to depend on.

> **It's a painful process, but it's good.**

So in your discouragement, remember that your challenging circumstances are a great reason to relish your high position. They are putting you in a position of depending on God, a priceless skill for now and eternity.

2. Get God's perspective on your <u>future</u>.

How? By looking at your future through the lens of *hope*. If our hope is in the here and now, the tangible and visible, no matter what it is—money in the bank, affirmation from other people, favorable situations, or whatever—it rises and falls by the day or even the minute. But the hope God offers us is constant. He gives us a new set of glasses so we can see past whatever is discouraging us and into the hope of eternity.

Here's what the apostle Paul had to say about our hope:

> We do not lose heart. Though outwardly we are wasting away, yet inwardly we are being renewed day by day. For our light and momentary troubles are achieving for us an eternal glory that far outweighs them all. So we fix our eyes not on what is seen, but on what is unseen, since what is seen is temporary, but what is unseen is eternal. (2 Corinthians 4:16-18)

Paul had been shipwrecked, beaten, imprisoned, persecuted, abandoned, and slandered and had gone through all sorts of hardships, yet he recognized that troubles are "momentary" and eternal glory "outweighs them all." If you are a believer in Jesus, you will never go through painful circumstances that aren't worth it. In the kingdom of God, the benefits always outweigh the costs. That's God's perspective on your future.

3. Get God's perspective on your <u>motivation</u>.

How? By looking at your motivation through the lens of *love*.

I taught a seminar in Hong Kong years ago and met with a group of pastors for dinner afterward. One of the pastors was a house-church leader who was telling us how he had used some of the resources we had given him.

He told a story of being away on an evangelistic trip while his church was meeting in his home. Officials from the Communist Party came, and this pastor's wife got all the church members to leave and told the officials that she was the pastor and that no one else was there. They took her to the police station and kept her there for two days, during which she was beaten, until her husband returned from his trip.

As I was listening to this, I couldn't help feeling angry and vengeful. I kept thinking about how I would respond if someone did that to my wife. I wasn't even sure I could keep my faith if God allowed her to go through that.

But when this pastor finished his story, he calmly looked at me and a friend who was traveling with me and said, "Can you imagine that God would count us worthy to suffer for Him?" (In that moment, I realized how "American" my faith was.)

That man's attitude toward suffering was the response of Peter and John when they were dragged before the court of the Sanhedrin and beaten for doing miracles and preaching about Jesus. They left "rejoicing because they had been counted worthy of suffering disgrace for the Name" (Acts 5:41).

> Remembering that our endurance expresses our love is a powerful antidote to discouragement.

Like Paul, they wanted to know the fellowship of Jesus's suffering (Philippians 3:10). They were motivated by loyalty and love.

Our love for Jesus is precious to God, but it's especially precious when we refuse to give up in suffering because we love Him and want to be like Him. I have to admit that I've often felt discouraged and impatient when I've worked hard on what I believe God has called me to do and things aren't working out how I expected them to. Sometimes my motivation seems to be more about God working things out in my life rather than my being willing to experience hardship as an expression of love for Him.

Are you motivated by love? That's a sobering question and a deeply personal one, and the way we answer it is unique to each of us. But it's an important one to consider. Remembering that our endurance expresses our love is a powerful antidote to discouragement.

You Are Not a Victim

Remember, there's a big difference between victims and survivors. Victims look through the lenses of "me" and "now." Their issue is whether things are going well for them or not. Survivors look through the lenses we've discussed in this chapter. They count it all joy, ask for God's wisdom, see from an eternal perspective, and are motivated by love. With the perspective of a survivor, you have everything you need to overcome discouragement.

But you will have to fight it. Remember when I asked you to read this chapter with your most discouraging situation in mind? How can you know if you're viewing that specific situation through the lenses of faith, hope, and love? Ask yourself three diagnostic questions.

1. Is my faith in things that are <u>perishable</u> or in things that are <u>permanent</u>?

Reevaluate your circumstances in light of that question. What are you actually trusting in: things that last or things that don't?

I met a Chinese pastor many years ago who had been beaten and tortured. His church grew. The authorities later put him in prison, and his church grew even more. Finally, they showed up while he was preaching, with hundreds of people gathered around listening, and they told him they were going to kill him.

His response was full of faith: "You torture me, the church grows. You imprison me, the church grows even bigger. You kill me, the church will multiply beyond your wildest imagination." After consideration, the authorities decided he was probably right and left him alone. His faith was not in what was perishable; it was in what was permanent.

I've been inspired by many people who look at life that same way. I know of an Iranian woman who came to a training session recently, and when it was time for her to return to her home country, which is very oppressive toward Christians, she asked the trainer if he could also teach her how to "die well," as she knew that attending the training would likely cost her her life.

Last year I sat across the table from a young doctor from Yemen who had a contract on her life. She matter-of-factly told me that she probably wouldn't live very long but that her calling was more important than her life. I have a mentor here in the U.S. who made a lot of money and then lost it and made it back again several times. He took another hit during recent instability in the stock market. But when I asked him how he was doing financially, he simply said, "It really doesn't matter. It's just money."

These people understand that trials, losses, setbacks, and hardships can't make or break you. Their eyes are set on bigger things.

2. Is my hope determined by the size of my <u>problems</u> or the certainty of God's <u>promises</u>?

Reevaluate where your focus is. Are you hoping your problems will go away, or are you putting your hope in the long-term purposes and plans of God? Do your problems seem huge and God small, or vice versa? Where is your focus?

Paul emphasized hope at the end of his letter to the Romans, who were going through a few struggles of their own. He reminded them that everything written in the past—that is, the Old Testament—was to teach us "so that through the endurance taught in the Scriptures and the encouragement they provide we might have hope" (Romans 15:4).

He wrote about "the God who gives endurance and encouragement" (Romans 15:5) and then gave them this blessing: "May the God of hope fill you with all joy and peace as you trust in him, so that you may overflow with hope by the power of the Holy Spirit" (Romans 15:13). God wants to bring us to a place of dependence that enables us to endure. How? Through the truth of Scripture.

In a crisis, does your mind focus on the problem or the promise? That's a choice. We all have strong mental habits, but we can change them. We can choose to be filled with hope.

3. Is my primary motivation to <u>love Christ</u> or to simply <u>experience relief</u>?

It isn't always easy to answer that question. But when I look at the many believers around the world who serve God in spite of the suffering they know they will experience, I see pictures of love. They are willing to endure hardship for the One who sacrificed His life for them.